Face Painting

Face Painting

From cowboys to clowns, pirates
to princesses, 40 amazingly
original designs for the perfect
children's party

LYNSY PINSENT

CHARTWELL
BOOKS, INC.

A QUINTET BOOK

Published by Chartwell Books
A Division of Book Sales, Inc.
110 Enterprise Avenue
Secaucus, New Jersey 07094

This edition produced for sale in the U.S.A.,
its territories and dependencies only.

ISBN 1-55521-918-7

This book was designed and produced by
Quintet Publishing Limited
6 Blundell Street
London N7 9BH

Creative Director: Richard Dewing
Designer: Ian Hunt
Project Editor: Katie Preston
Editor: Jenny Millington
Picture Research: Lynsy Pinsent
Photographers: Paul Forrester and Chas Wilder

Typeset in Great Britain by
Central Southern Typesetters, Eastbourne
Manufactured in Singapore by Colour Trend
Printed in Singapore by
Star Standard Industries (Pte) Ltd

Contents

Introduction

Body decoration has been used for over 40,000 years all over the world and for many different purposes. In the Western world it may be used to make a statement, for example by a punk rocker who wants to challenge society, to follow fashion or enhance looks, by performers in the theatre or circus, or simply for fun.

In other societies, the way in which a body is decorated instantly distinguishes between race, tribe, class and age. In all parts of the world, those who do not conform to the norm risk rejection by society. However, the more "primitive" cultures use pattern and paint for rituals and celebrations and to symbolize their physical and spiritual being.

ABOVE: Nadia Strahan making up as Bombalurina in Andrew Lloyd Webber's musical Cats.

ABOVE: Red is a significant colour for many tribes. It is mostly connected with blood, life, energy, success and well being. Upon marriage, women of many Asian and Middle Eastern countries, for example Bahrein, tint their hands and feet with red henna to invite success and good health to the home.

RIGHT: Before going to war, some North American Indians painted red around their eyes and ears to invoke good luck in hearing and vision. They wanted to frighten their enemies and receive protection from the spirit world. In contrast, a modern soldier's "war paint" is designed to keep him from view.

ABOVE: *The Japanese Kabuki theatre and Chinese Opera (shown here) are not simply forms of entertainment, they also follow ancient rituals and traditions within the performances, costumes and make-up. The dramas performed are based on traditional legends. Specific colours and designs are assigned to particular types of characters.*

ABOVE: *For the Mount Hagen people of Papua New Guinea, body decoration is a vital element of their culture. They are a fiercely competitive society and try to ensure their decorations meet the approval of their elders. The picture shows a tribesman decorated for the pig festival.*

Equipment

For the designs in this book you will need the following:

EQUIPMENT

Aqua-Colours (water-based paints in a range of colours)
Black eye pencil
Bran flakes or cornflakes
Brushes
Cotton buds
Derma Wax (or "nose putty")
Fake blood
Glitter gel for skin
Grey eye pencil
Hair brush & comb
Hair clips/hair band
Hair gel
Hairspray
Lead pencil
Mirror
Palette knife/spatula
Soap
Sponges
Tissues
Toothpick/orange stick
Towel
Tracing paper (or greaseproof paper)
Water
Water jar

Note: All the paints recommended in this book are professional Aqua-Colours. These are specially formulated for use on skin, are non-toxic and have been carefully tested. However, if you suspect that your model might have sensitive skin, test the paint on the inside of the model's wrist before you begin. If there is no reaction after an hour or two you should be safe to proceed.

Aqua-Colours

The main advantages of using professional Aqua-Colours are that they cover the skin well, yet only need a thin layer of paint to do so. They are available in a huge range of colours that can be mixed easily and dry very quickly on the skin, enabling other colours to be added almost immediately.

Because Aqua-Colours are water based they are easily removed by washing with ordinary soap and water, and can also be used on the hair for the same reason.

Aqua-Colours are inexpensive and can be bought individually or in palettes of 6 or 12 colours. Fluorescent colours are also available. A list of suppliers can be found on page 96.

Brushes and Sponges

Special make-up sponges can be bought from most chemist shops, but an ordinary bath sponge will do the job just as well, if not better sometimes.

A professional "stipple" sponge is good for applying beard stubble, but a plastic pan scourer will produce the same effect.

A selection of quality brushes are essential for a good make-up. The most useful are: No. 2 for eye-lining and fine detail; No. 6 for lips and eyes; 6mm (¼in) domed for highlights and blending; 12mm (½in) domed for painting large areas and for blending.

The best type of brushes are sable, although other, cheaper types can be used instead. Sable brushes

ABOVE: Equipment for achieving special effects.

are worth the extra initial expense because they are versatile and long lasting. Look after them carefully by washing them gently with soap and water after each session, then lubricating the hairs with a touch of cold cream. Your local art shop will be a good source of brushes.

Preparation Tips

☞ Set out all your materials and equipment in front of you so that you can see at a glance what you need.

☞ Lay out a towel or cloth to protect the table or work surface.

☞ Keep a waste bin or carrier bag handy to hold dirty tissues etc. and keep the work area clear.

☞ Try to ensure that your model sits on a seat that is high enough for you to work comfortably without straining your back.

☞ Have a mirror close at hand, preferably standing in front of you, so that you can check that your make-up design is balanced and the colours are evenly applied.

☞ Before you start, wrap a towel round your model's shoulders to protect the clothes.

☞ Keep the model's hair off the face with hair clips or a hair band.

☞ Have a good supply of cotton buds handy for blending colours and erasing any smudges.

☞ Most important of all, work out your designs beforehand using a copy of the make-up chart on page 15. It is much better to make your mistakes on paper rather than a model's face! The chart will also be a useful record for future use.

Application Tips

☞ Always begin with a clean, dry face.

☞ For some designs you might find it helpful to sketch the outline onto the face first using grey eye pencil.

☞ When a full white base is required, try to apply it as thinly as possible while still achieving good coverage – this will avoid muddiness when other colours are added.

☞ Do not apply glitter too close to the eyes.

☞ When using Derma Wax (or nose putty) don't handle it for too long or it will become too sticky to use.

☞ Fake blood can be darkened by adding a little instant coffee, and can be made less orange or pink by adding a touch of green.

☞ Fake blood can stain clothing – take great care with it.

☞ When painting animal faces, it often helps to keep a photograph of the animal nearby. This will inspire you to imitate the real thing as accurately as possible.

☞ Keep each sponge for one colour only – washing sponges between colours takes up too much time.

☞ Change the water often.

☞ Always apply the lightest colours first, then progress to the darker ones.

☞ Wait until the previous colour is dry before applying the next one.

☞ Blend colours with a clean, damp brush or by stippling with a barely damp sponge.

☞ Take extra care when working near the eyes. If possible, ask the model to keep their eyes closed until you have finished.

☞ Always apply make-up with as much care as possible. Do not rush – the features will become ill-defined and uneven. Symmetrical shapes and neat lines are the essence of a good make-up. Practice makes perfect!

Basic Techniques

Applying a Base

TIP: Use a damp sponge to apply a full-face base. It is much quicker and gives a smoother finish than a brush. To avoid streaks or patchiness, make sure the sponge is not too wet.

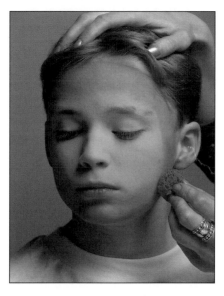

3 Blend an orange border into the yellow by lightly dabbing ("stippling") along the adjoining edge with a barely damp sponge.

TIP: Dark skins can sometimes be difficult to cover. Stipple the base colour over the entire face with a barely damp sponge. Metallic colours can be substituted, and look terrific. They also act as a primer onto which you can apply your base colour.

4 The finished duotone base.

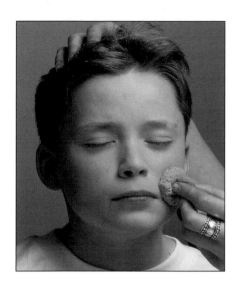

1 If you want a duotone base, always apply the lightest colour first – yellow in this case.

2 The yellow base reaches almost to the hairline.

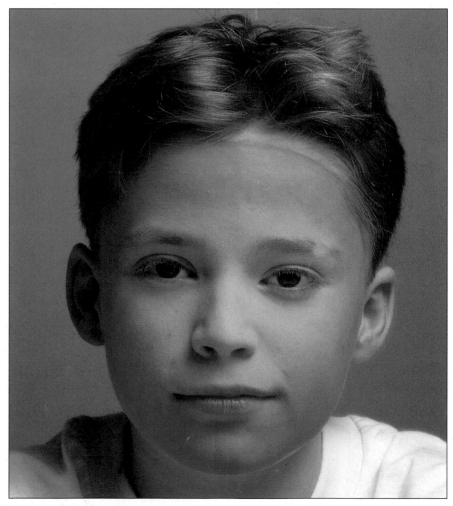

Painting the Eyes

TIP: Always take great care when painting anywhere near the eye. Most of the faces in this book have been designed so that the models can keep their eyes closed throughout the whole procedure. If you need to get closer to the bottom eye-line, ask the model to look up and away from the brush as you do so.

Method 1

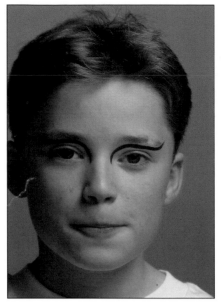

1 This method is ideal for very young children because it starts beside the nose and sweeps across the brow without actually touching the eye.

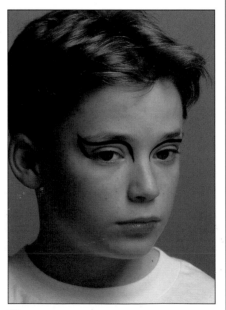

2 You can enhance the effect by simply bringing the end of the line down to meet the outer corner of the eye.

Method 2

1 For a more elaborate image, use a thin brush and start the top line just below the inner corner of the eye.

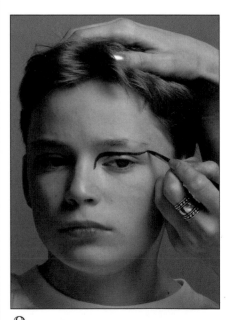

2 Take the line across the eyelid, winging it up slightly at the end.

3 Bring the end of the top line down to the outer corner of the eye.

5 Start the bottom line at the inner corner and sweep it beneath the lower lashes to join the outer corner of the top lid.

1 Shape the top lid using the method described previously.

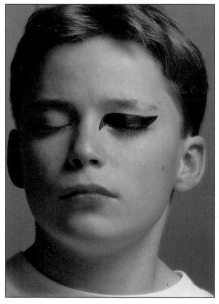

4 Fill in the outlined area in black.

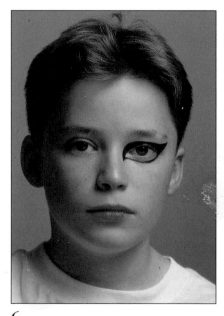

6 The finished effect.

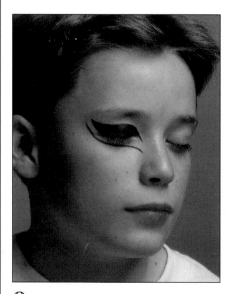

2 Start the lower line below the inner corner and sweep it up, following the direction of the top lid, to finish parallel to but not touching the top line. The space between the two lines can be emphasised with a slick of white paint.

☞ This "open-ended" technique is often used in the theatre because it makes the eyes appear larger.

Five O'Clock Shadow

1 To create an unshaven look, use a small coarse sponge to stipple black/brown paint gently over the beard and moustache area of the face.

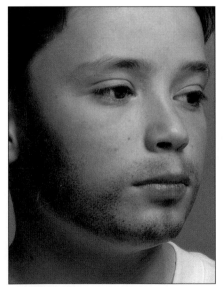

2 The finished effect.

TIP: Build up the depth of colour very gradually. Tap the sponge on the back of your hand before each application of colour to remove any excess paint. If any areas start to look too dark, stipple them lightly with a paler colour.

Eyebrows

A change of eyebrow shape can transform a face into a multitude of different characters. Think about the type of personality you are trying to convey. Make faces in the mirror – of laughter, anger, sadness – and see what happens to your features. Build up a repertoire of shapes based on what you observe.

1. Sad.

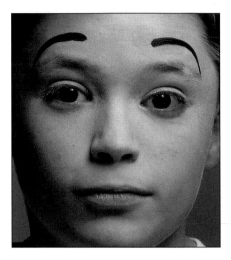

2. Surprised.

3. Cruel.

Using a Make-up Chart – A Finished Example

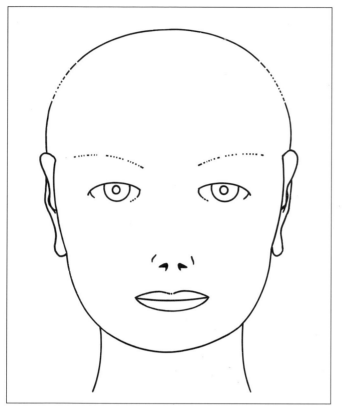

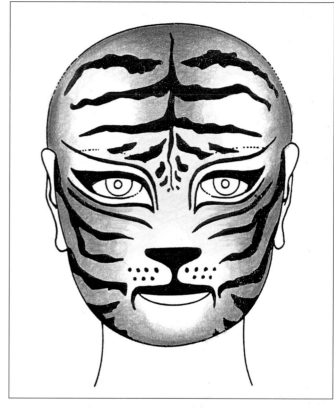

1 You can photocopy this blank chart to help you plan your own creations.

2 Fill in the design with paints, felt tips or coloured pencils.

3 Keep referring to your chart as you apply the make-up.

1
ANIMALS

From time immemorial, people the world over have painted their faces and bodies to imitate animals; either to enhance their physical appearance or perhaps with the hope of acquiring some of the amazing powers of the natural world.

The young men of the Nuba tribes in South-eastern Sudan paint their bodies purely for decoration. The animals represented are chosen for their elegance and beauty rather than their spiritual and physical powers.

In most tribal societies, however, people believe that by painting the body with the stripes of a tiger, for example, or by wearing the feathers of an eagle they will assume the strength and grace of these creatures and increase their own powers beyond their natural limit.

Leopard

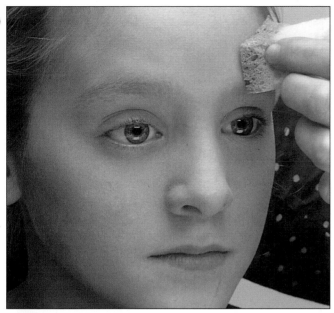

1 Dab yellow base colour over the whole of the face using a sponge.

2 Use another sponge to shade the outer parts of the face with mid-brown.

3 Merge the two colours together by stippling gently with the yellow sponge.

TIP: When stippling colours to blend them, keep the sponge almost dry; squeeze it onto a tissue to remove any excess moisture.

4 Stipple white paint with a sponge over the mouth and chin, and from each eyebrow up to the hairline.

5 With a thin brush, paint black across the whole eyelid. Start at the inner corner of the eye, take the line past the outer corner and wing it up slightly at the end.
☐ Paint a black line down from the inner corner of the eye and over the cheek.
☐ Paint a black line below the bottom eyelashes, starting at the inner nose line. Follow the direction of the top lid, sweeping the end of the lower line up to meet it at the outer corner.

6 Paint the tip of the nose black. Draw a thin line from the centre of the nose down to the top lip. Paint the top lip only in black, dropping the ends down at each corner of the mouth. Block out the bottom lip completely with white.

7 Already the model has a real animal look; this is because the main features of the face – the eyes, nose and mouth – have been de-humanised to a large extent. Once this effect has been achieved, the image is set, and any further decoration is incidental. This is why you must follow the preliminary stages so carefully.

8 Having added the whisker spots to the top lip with black, paint on some leopard markings in very dark brown, highlighting them just off-centre with flecks of white.

9 Remember, most animal markings are symmetical.

10 The finished leopard.

Lion

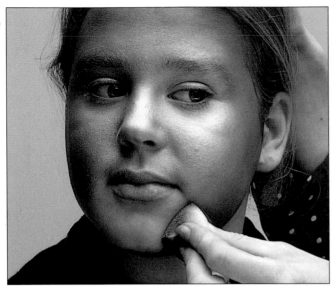

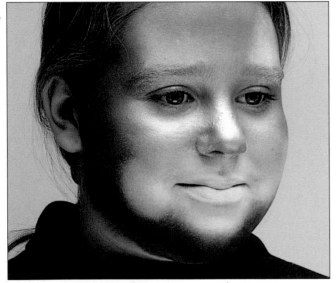

1 The base of this make-up is gold, with dark brown around the edges of the face. Apply the colours with sponges and stipple to blend them together.

2 Using a clean sponge, stipple white paint over each eyebrow, fading it out towards the hairline. Apply the white to the mouth and chin as well, extending it across the cheeks to create a heavy-jowled look.

3 Paint the whole eyelid black, taking the colour underneath the eye and a little way down the side of the nose. Blend the eye colour into the base with fine, sharp brush strokes. This technique is known as "feathering".

□ The nose and mouth are created in the same way as the leopard (see page 18), but allowing the mouth lines to extend further down the chin to outline and emphasise the lion's jowls.

4 Decorate the outer edges of the face with rough, intermittent lines in dark red. Repeat these lines in very dark brown or black.

Add some black whiskers, and the lion is finished.

Tiger

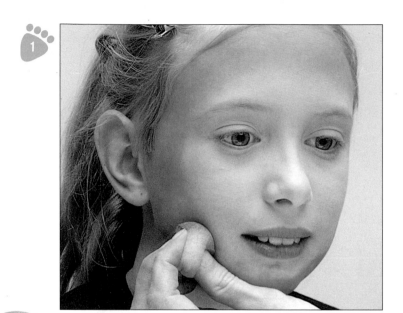

1 Apply a base of yellow with orange on the outer edges. Stipple the colours together with a sponge.

2 Stipple on white patches around the mouth and above the eyebrows. Paint the eyes in black, starting just below the inner corner; take the colour across the lid and wing the line up slightly just past the outer corner of the eye. Paint the lower eyeline below the lashes, following the curve of the top line but leaving the outer end open.

▯ The mouth and nose are applied in the same way as for the leopard (see page 18) except that the tiger's nose should be extended a little way onto the cheek.

3 For the tiger's stripes, use a narrow brush to paint black lines across the forehead. Finish one side of the face first, then copy the design onto the other side to keep the pattern symmetrical.

4 The finished tiger. Because the markings are so strong, there is no need to add whiskers — these would only clutter the face and spoil the effect.

Dog

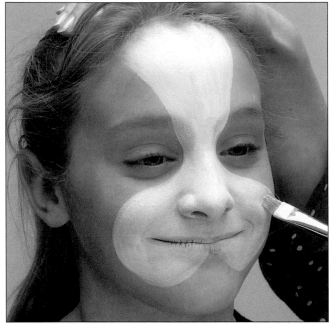

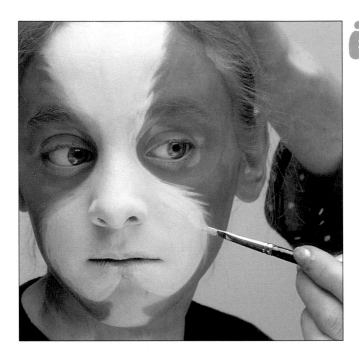

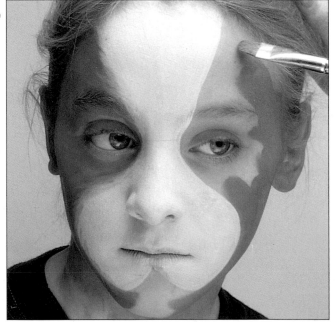

1 Using a flat, wide brush, paint this white shape down the centre of the face.

2 Fill in around the white with a mid-brown.

3 Soften the line where the two colours meet by feathering the white onto the brown with a very fine brush.

4 Paint the eyes in dark brown, using jagged, uneven brush strokes.

5 Use black for the mouth, extending the line beyond the corners of the mouth before dropping it down sharply to the chin. Paint the tip of the nose black and add some black whisker spots.

6 The drooping tongue is dark red. Fleck the eye areas with red and yellow to highlight them.

Rabbit

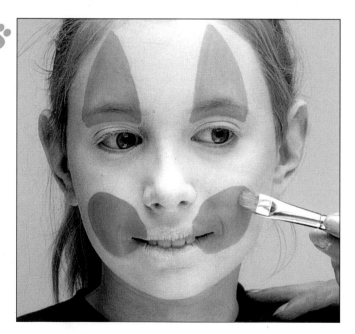

1 Use a sponge to apply white to the whole face.

2 Paint pink circles over the corners of the mouth onto the cheeks and pink eye shapes from the eyebrows to the hairline using a wide, flat brush.

3 Outline the eye shapes with thin purple lines. Extend the bottom lines down the nose a little and sweep the outer ends up towards the temples.

4 Tell the model to close her eyes, and draw a fine slanted purple line underneath the bottom eyelashes. Colour the end of the nose purple, and join it to the mouth with a thin purple line. Outline the natural shape of the model's lips in purple leaving the middle third of the bottom lip free.

5 Draw the outline of the teeth over the bottom lip, using a very fine brush and black paint. Fill in the teeth with white. Add some small black whisker spots, and carefully draw in the fine blue whiskers and brow detail.

6 Paint a neat white line around the inside of the brow shapes to emphasise them.

7 The finished rabbit.

Glam-Cat

1 Cover the face with white paint blended into a red border by stippling with a damp sponge.

2 Paint the upper eyeline in black, starting just below the inner corner of the eye, following the lash line and sweeping the end of the line out and up. The lower line is also black, and follows the curve of the upper one, sweeping up to join it at the outer edge. Fill in the whole eyelid area in black.

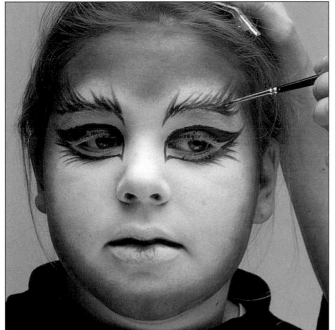

3 Use small, delicate brush strokes to create the eyebrows, making sure their shape follows that of the eyelines. Paint in some similar lines along the outer edge of the lower eyeline.

4 Paint the tip of the nose black, taking the centre line down to the top lip. Paint along the top lip and curl the ends of the line up slightly onto the cheek. Add black whisker spots.

5 Around the edge of the face, apply some rough strokes of grey. Highlight this shaggy effect, and the area below the eyebrow, with patchy dashes of yellow. Draw a small dark red semicircle on the bottom lip.

6 A very glamorous cat.

Black Cat

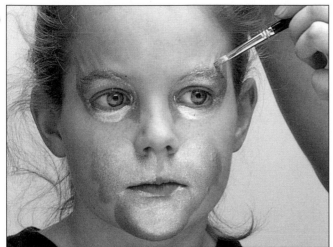

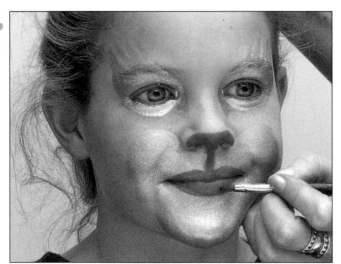

1 Paint silver around the mouth, chin and eyes, making these areas slightly larger than they will eventually be.

2 Square off the end of the nose in pink, and apply the same colour to the lips.

3 Carefully paint round the silver features in black, then fill in the rest of the face.

4 Using a fine brush and sharp, delicate strokes, feather the black paint onto the silver to give a softer, more textured effect.

5 Add black whisker spots, followed by white whiskers and white eyebrow details. Because the paint is easily removed by washing, the colours can be extended into the hair to complete the make-up.

6 The finished black cat.

Eyes on Eyelids

Ask the model to close her eyes, then paint the upper eyelids yellow, outline the eye socket with a thin line of black and paint a black iris in the centre.

Magic Cat

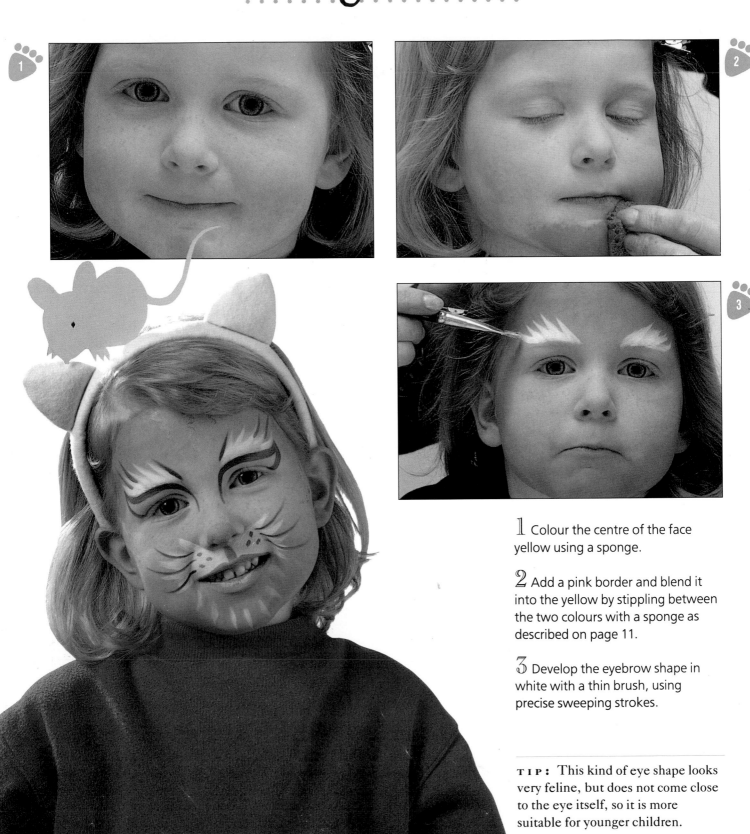

1 Colour the centre of the face yellow using a sponge.

2 Add a pink border and blend it into the yellow by stippling between the two colours with a sponge as described on page 11.

3 Develop the eyebrow shape in white with a thin brush, using precise sweeping strokes.

TIP: This kind of eye shape looks very feline, but does not come close to the eye itself, so it is more suitable for younger children.

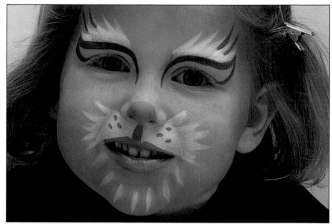

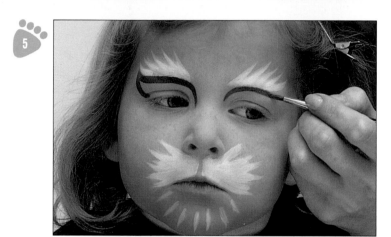

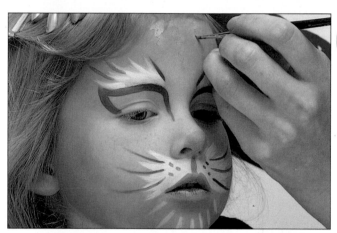

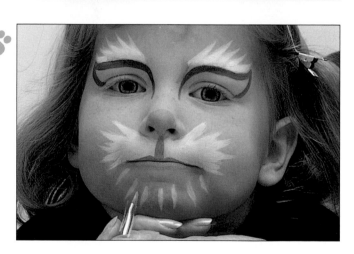

4 Paint white whiskery fluff above the top lip in the same way, adding a few flecks of white to the chin.

5 The eye shapes are outlined in purple, starting beside the nose and sweeping the line along the brow-bone.

6 Paint the tip of the nose lilac and bring the colour down onto the mouth to enhance its natural shape.

7 Use a very fine brush to add blue whisker spots and some brow details.

8 With the same brush, paint a streak of dark red above the inner end of each brow line and add a few delicate red whiskers.

9 Complete the make-up with a few bright green squiggles on the forehead and cheeks.

Frog

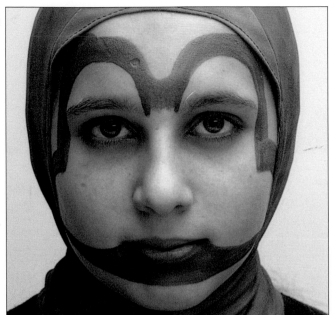

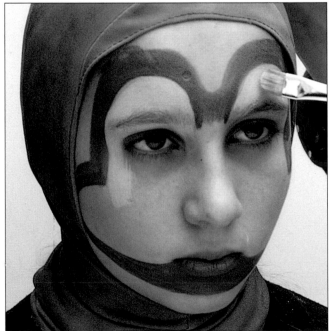

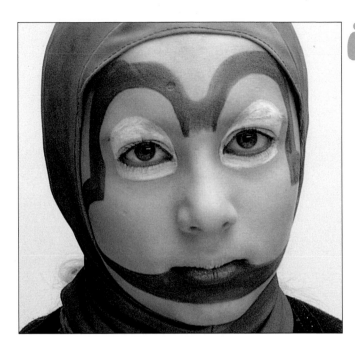

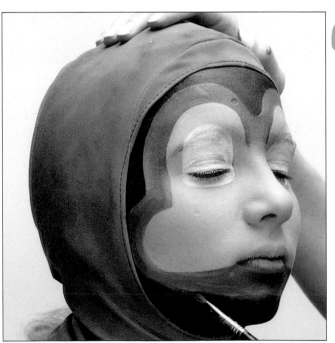

1 The basic outline is applied in green, with the cheek lines extending right out to the ears.

2 Fill the area inside the green lines with yellow, using a flat, wide brush.

3 Leaving a rim of yellow, paint white patches underneath and around the eyes.

4 Paint in the area outside the green lines with a very dark brown.

5 Following the edge of the green, draw a thick black line across the top lip from one side of the face to the other.

TIP: Outline the black mouth with white to make it seem more protruberant.

6 Use a cotton bud to mottle the nose and cheeks with pale brown.

Zebra

TIP: As the markings of a zebra are so repetitive, it is a very good idea to draw this design on a copy of the make-up chart (see page 15) before you begin. This will give you something to refer to if the lines begin to confuse you!

1 Cover the face and neck with white paint, using a sponge.

2 Stipple grey over the nose and mouth area.

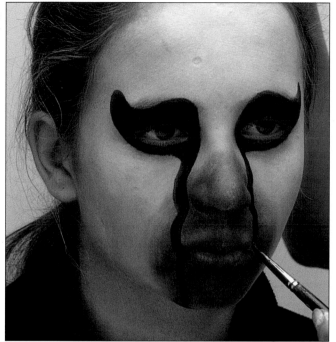

3 Paint the black shapes over the eyes, extending the inner corners right down past the sides of the nose and onto the chin.

4 Draw a rough line down the middle of the forehead and use this as a centre point for the rest of the black markings on the forehead and down the nose.

5 For the zebra, it is easier to work on both sides of the face at the same time, rather than completing one side first. You will find it less confusing, and it will be easier to keep the pattern symmetrical.

6 The finished zebra.

Ladybird

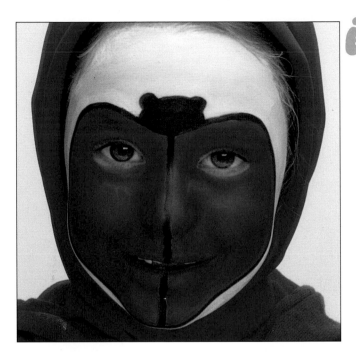

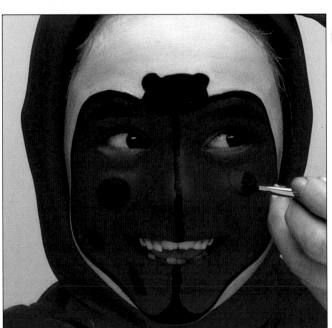

1 Using a thin brush, carefully paint the black outline onto the face.

TIP: It might help to draw the shape onto the face with a grey eye pencil first.

2 Fill in the shape with red, using a flat, wide brush.

3 Paint the borders of the face in white, taking great care not to let the colours overlap.

4 Add the black spots and a small black triangle on the chin.

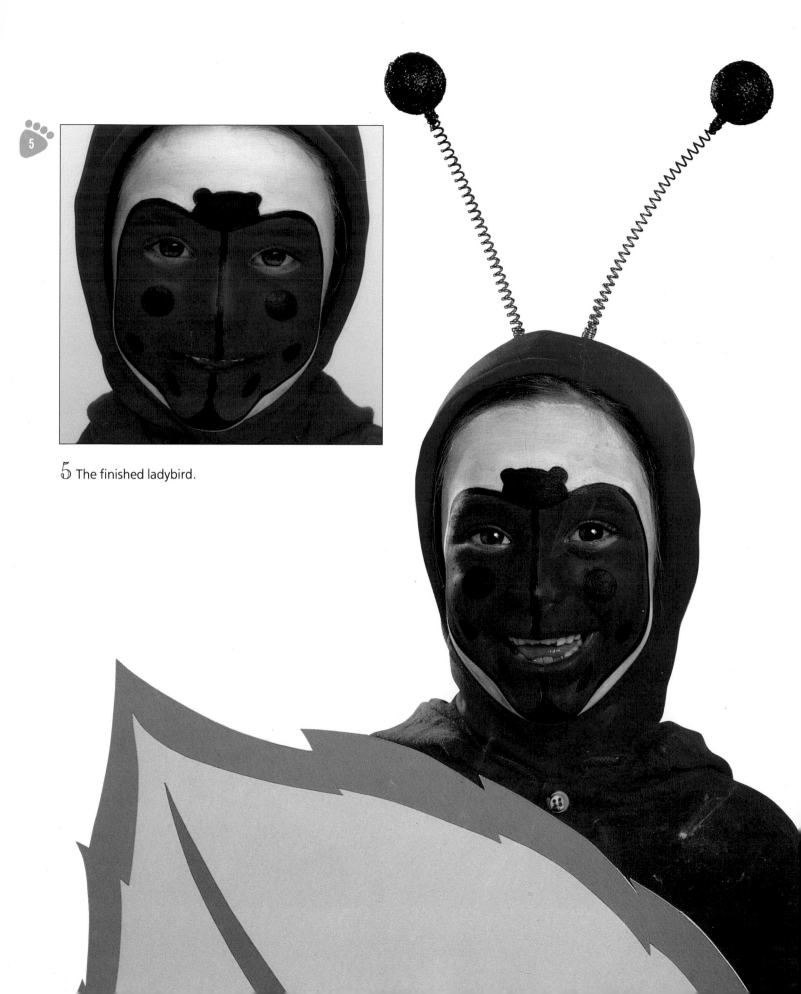

5 The finished ladybird.

2
CLOWNS

The history of the clown is a surprisingly long one – the role dates back over 4000 years, to well before there were such things as circuses. In their earliest days, the clown figures were known as jesters, fools, buffoons or gleemen, and they entertained the crowds at fairs, markets or in other public places. They were also employed by the nobility to entertain private guests, at the Royal Court for example.

Today there are three main types of clown: the Hobo or Tramp, the Auguste, and the White Face. The most well-known Hobo or Tramp clown is probably Charlie Chaplin. The Auguste type of clown is the zaniest of the three and wears the most bizarre and exaggerated make-up. The White Face clown is the graceful, thoughtful one, of which a popular example is the Pierrot.

The Pierrot clown is sometimes known as Pedrolino, and can be traced back to early 17th-century Italy, but the romantic figure we associate with the name today was created in the 19th century by the French mime artist Jean Baptiste Gaspard Deburau. Traditionally Pierrot is sad because the dashing Harlequin has stolen his true love, Columbine – this is the cause of the single tear that always appears under one eye.

Pierrot

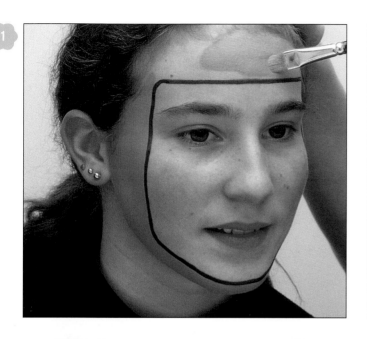

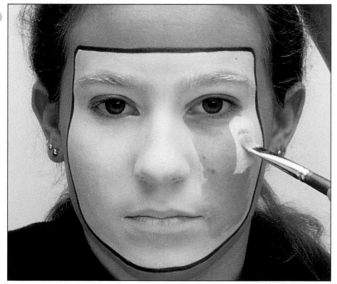

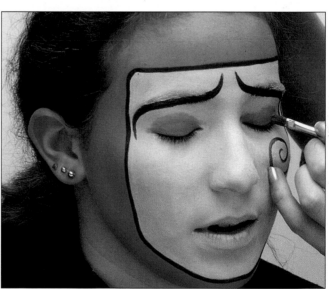

1 You will need a steady hand to paint this outline onto the face; try to keep the line as sharp and even as possible. It might help to draw the shape onto the face with grey eye pencil first before painting the line in black. Paint the area outside the mask in pink using a wide, flat brush.

2 Rinse the flat brush and use it to fill in the mask area in white, taking great care not to go over the black outline. If any white areas seem patchy or streaky, stipple over them gently with a sponge.

3 The eyebrows are an essential part of Pierrot's sad expression. Start the brow line quite high above the

natural eyebrow, then drop the line down diagonally to end below the outer corner of the eye. One side has a decorative curl.

4 Paint the eyelids in the same shade of pink as the edges of the face.

5 Use a very fine brush to paint a thick black line across the upper eyelid next to the lashes, ending a little way beyond the outer corner of the eye.

6 With the same brush, paint a thin black line under the bottom row of eyelashes, again extending the line to just beyond the outer corner of the eye. This will make the eye seem larger.

7 Cover the lips with white and paint in the lip shape in black with a very fine brush. You could use a fine black eye pencil if you prefer.

8 Colour the lips pink.

9 Paint the essential Pierrot tears carefully onto one cheek in black.

10 You can add some silver glitter to the teardrops to give them a watery look, or they could be coloured in blue. For extra glamour, add a few dots of silver glitter to the lips and brows.

11 Poor Pierrot.

Baby Clown

1 Paint on a wide red smile, and add a red dot on each cheek and a red tip to the nose.

2 Outline the red mouth shape with yellow. With the model's eyes closed, add a blue triangle under each eye. Make the nose and cheek markings look shiny with some white highlights.

3 Using a thin brush, paint on some arched purple eyebrows and a dash of purple above each eye.

4 A very cheerful clown face.

Funny Clown

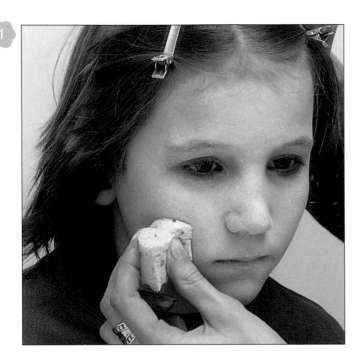

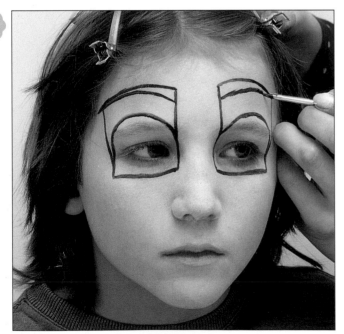

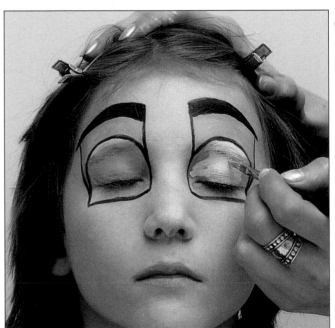

1 Cover the whole face in white paint using a sponge. Stipple lightly over any patches that seem streaky to make a really smooth finish.

2 Draw in the main eye shapes with a very fine brush, and add the eyebrows.

3 Fill in the eyebrows in black. The space underneath each one is filled in with blue.

4 Cover the main eye area carefully in white.

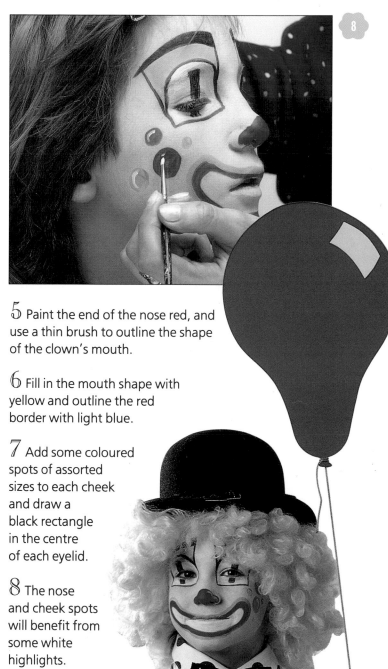

5 Paint the end of the nose red, and use a thin brush to outline the shape of the clown's mouth.

6 Fill in the mouth shape with yellow and outline the red border with light blue.

7 Add some coloured spots of assorted sizes to each cheek and draw a black rectangle in the centre of each eyelid.

8 The nose and cheek spots will benefit from some white highlights.

Card Clown

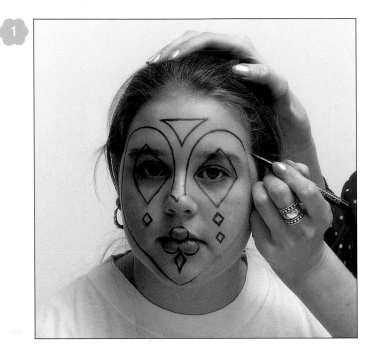

1 Sketch the design lightly onto the face with a grey eye pencil. Once you are satisfied that both sides of the face are even, trace over the design with either a very fine brush or a black liquid eyeliner pen.

2 Use a fine brush to make a white outline around all the inner shapes of the design.

3 Fill in the remaining areas with white.

4 Paint the diamond shapes black, including the eye shapes but leaving the eyelids blank.

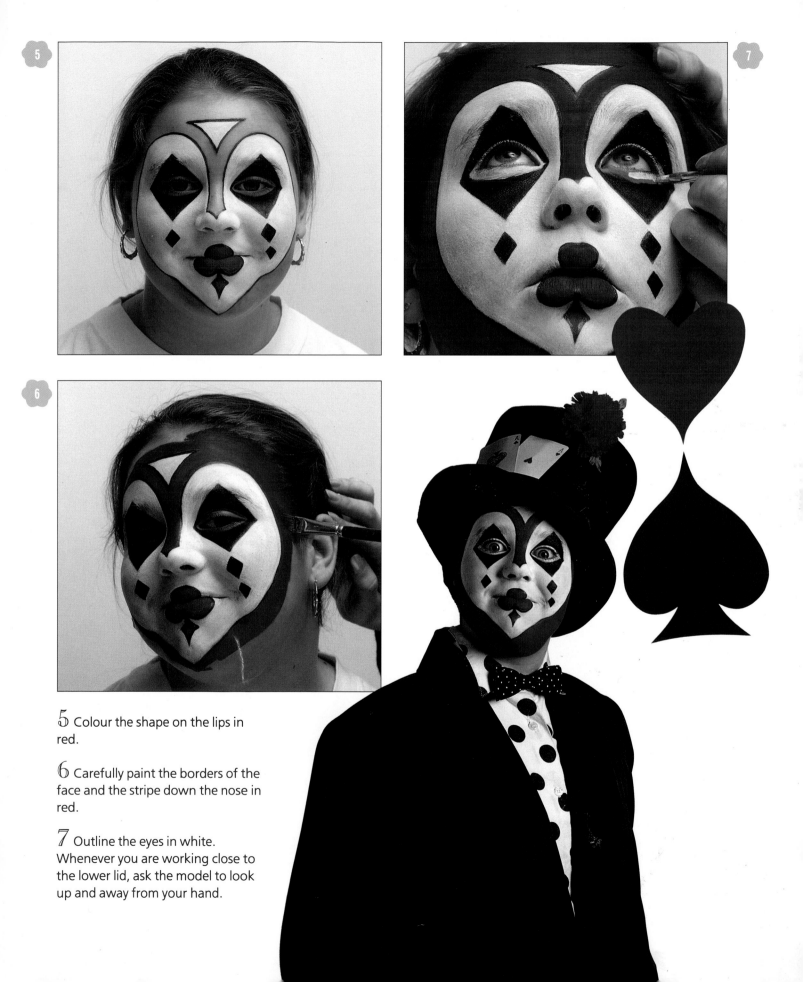

5 Colour the shape on the lips in red.

6 Carefully paint the borders of the face and the stripe down the nose in red.

7 Outline the eyes in white. Whenever you are working close to the lower lid, ask the model to look up and away from your hand.

3
HALLOWE'EN

Hallowe'en falls on 31 October – the day before the Christian Feast of Hallowmas or All Saints' Day. However, long before Christianity, it was a Pagan Festival called *Samhain*. 31 October marked the end of the Harvest and the Summer and the start of Winter and the Celtic New Year.

It was also on this night that witches and warlocks held their great *Sabbat*. People believed that on this night the gateway between the Supernatural world and this world was opened and that the spirits of the dead walked the earth. Gifts of food were left on doorsteps to appease restless ancestors and ritual bonfires were lit in the fields to keep evil spirits at bay. Turnip lanterns with menacing faces carved into them were hung outside houses to frighten away ghosts, and the people dressed up as demons or goblins with the belief that by imitating the other-worldly creatures, they would protect themselves from the powers of evil.

Devil

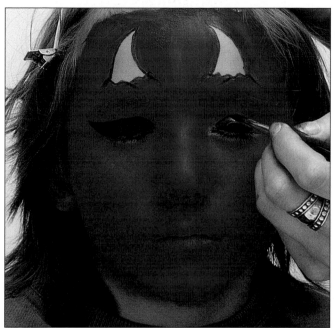

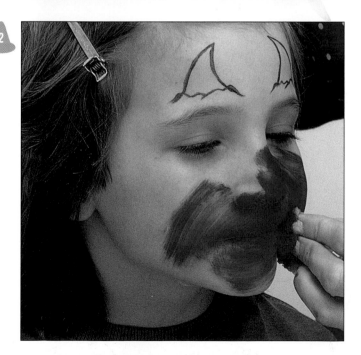

1 Sketch the horn shapes on the forehead with a very fine brush.

2 To keep a neat edge, use a brush to start painting the red area around the horns, then finish the rest of the face with a sponge.

3 Starting at the inner corner of the eye, paint the top lid black, winging the outer ends up slightly.

4 This may well be enough eye detail for younger children.

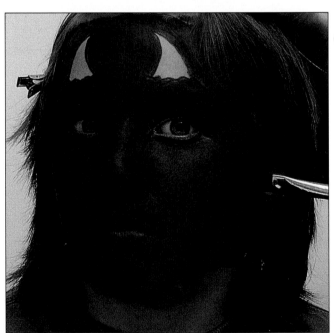

5 Add a thick black line under the bottom eyelashes, making a point at the inner corner and sweeping the line up to meet the top one at the outer corner.

6 Use black paint to make the nostrils look flared by extending them a little way up the nose.

7 The moustache and beard are built up with small sharp strokes of a fine brush, starting above the centre of the top lip.

8 Draw the eyebrows with the inner ends turned up into a frown. Add a line from the nose to the side of the mouth, following the natural crease in the model's cheek. Feel for the model's cheekbones, then enhance them by painting a black curve just below the bone. At a point beneath the centre of the eye, taper the line down onto the jawline.

9 Highlight the horns with gold paint and glitter.

10 A fearsome devil.

Pumpkin

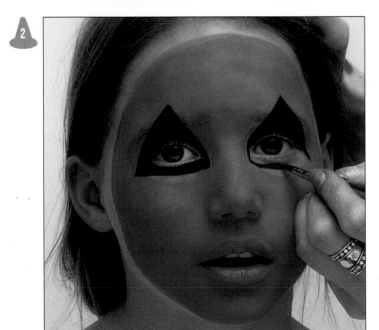

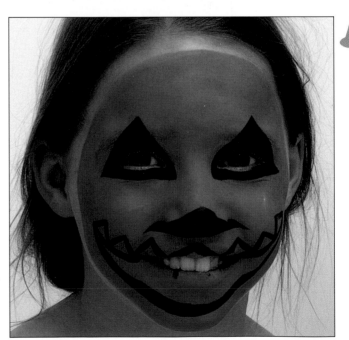

1 Paint a large orange circle over the whole face, filling in the colour with a sponge.

2 Add a black triangle over each eye, using a fine brush. Extend the points of the triangle below the line of the lower lid and carefully fill in the centre leaving a margin around the eye.

3 Paint another triangle on the tip of the nose and extend the sides out onto the cheeks.

4 Outline a huge smile in black and make the top edge a zig-zag line.

5 Fill in the whole mouth shape with black.

6 Design a small green stalk in the middle of the forehead and run some segment lines down from it, following the curve of the orange outline.

Wicked Witch

1 Paint the whole face white, stippling over any streaky areas with a sponge. Draw on the eyebrows with a very fine brush, taking the line up and away from the natural shape to form an arch. Turn the inner ends up to create a scowl.

2 Paint the eyelids black, starting at the inner corner of the eye and flicking the outer ends up towards the temples. Add a thin black line under the lower lashes, following the shape of the top line.

TIP: For safety, ask the model to close her eyes while you paint anywhere near them.

3 The lips are painted in luminous green. Add a line of the same green along the top edge of each eye.

4 On one side of the face, neatly draw three black lines that intersect.

5 Slowly and carefully develop the web pattern, keeping the lines as sharp as possible. Add the spider dangling on a thread — remember spiders have eight legs!

6 On the other cheek, draw a few stars and crescent shapes in black.

7 Decorate the eyebrows, lips and stars with gold or silver glitter.

Hag Witch

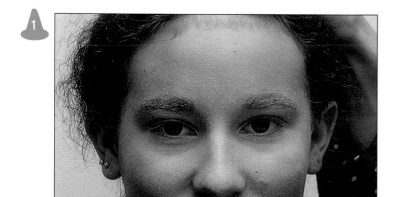

1 Use a sponge to cover the whole face in green. (Yellow or pale grey also work well for this make-up.)

2 Starting above the inner corner of the eye, paint a sharp diagonal line in black, sweeping up towards the temples. Feather the top edge of the line using small sharp strokes to suggest a coarse hairy eyebrow.

3 Paint the eyelids and inner corners of the eyes in dark brown, extending the colour down the sides of the nose to a point just above each nostril.

4 Start to create the folds and creases in the face; take the dark brown paint down along the folds of the cheeks to a point level with the mouth. Paint bags under the eyes by following the lower line of the eye socket at both the inner and outer corners. Feather all these lines with a damp brush.

TIP: When trying to age a young face, only apply lines in a downwards direction – lines that are drawn upwards will only lift the face and counteract the effect you are hoping for.

5 Add some creases across the forehead and two vertical frown lines. Blend these lines slightly with a cotton bud.

6 Paint some small wrinkles around the outer corners of the eyes and shade the hollows of the cheeks to make them look sunken.

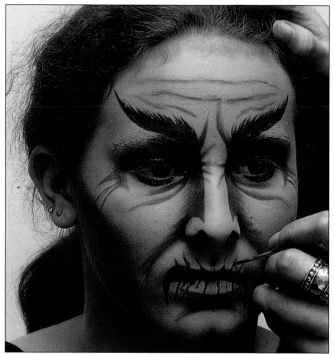

7 Small black semicircles on both top and bottom lids will give a beady-eyed look.

8 Block the mouth in green and draw a crooked black line across the lips, dropping the ends down at each corner of the mouth.

9 Add some fine wrinkle lines all round the mouth and a touch of shading to the cleft of the chin.

10 The hag witch is finished, and the model will hardly recognise herself!

Evil Queen

1 Use a sponge to colour the face and neck white, stippling gently over any streaky areas. Ignore the natural brow line – instead, create very exaggerated eyebrows that arch dramatically and turn up at the inner end forming a scowl.

2 Paint the whole eyelid and brow area in purple, joining the colour to the eyebrow line sharply at the outer corner of the eye.

3 Extend the purple right down each side of the nose, blending the outside edge away from the nose and into the base colour.

4 The frown has been accentuated by adding sharp-edged blocks of purple to the forehead with a slightly damp brush. Now paint the eyelids black, blending the line upwards onto the brow-bone and into the purple. The eye sockets now seem much deeper and the expression is suitably evil.

5 Draw a black line under the lower eyelashes starting just below the inner corner of the eye and sweeping up to end at the outer end of the eyebrow line.

6 Shade the hollows under the cheek bones with purple using a soft brush.

TIP: Aqua-Colours are sometimes tricky to blend, so you may prefer to use an ordinary powder eye shadow for this. However, powder shadows aren't usually recommended because they lack staying power and density of colour.

7 Give a sharp black outline to the lips with either a very fine brush or a sharp eye pencil. Fill the mouth shape in with purple.

8 The Evil Queen is finished.

Skull

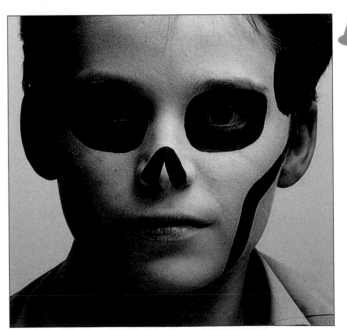

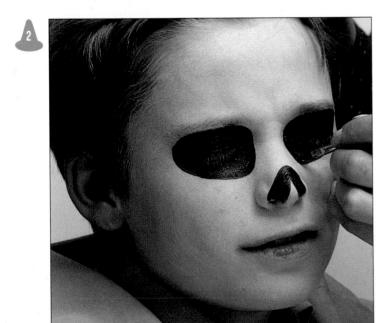

1 Cover the whole face in white using a sponge. Draw in the outlines for the nose and eye sockets in black.

2 Fill in these areas in black, leaving a small segment of white showing at the centre of the nose.

3 Feel for the model's temple hollows and emphasise them by painting a black semicircle over each one.

4 Feel for the cheekbones and paint along the underside, stopping approximately level with the centre of the eye. Then drop the line downwards to the jawline. Fill in the area behind this line with black.

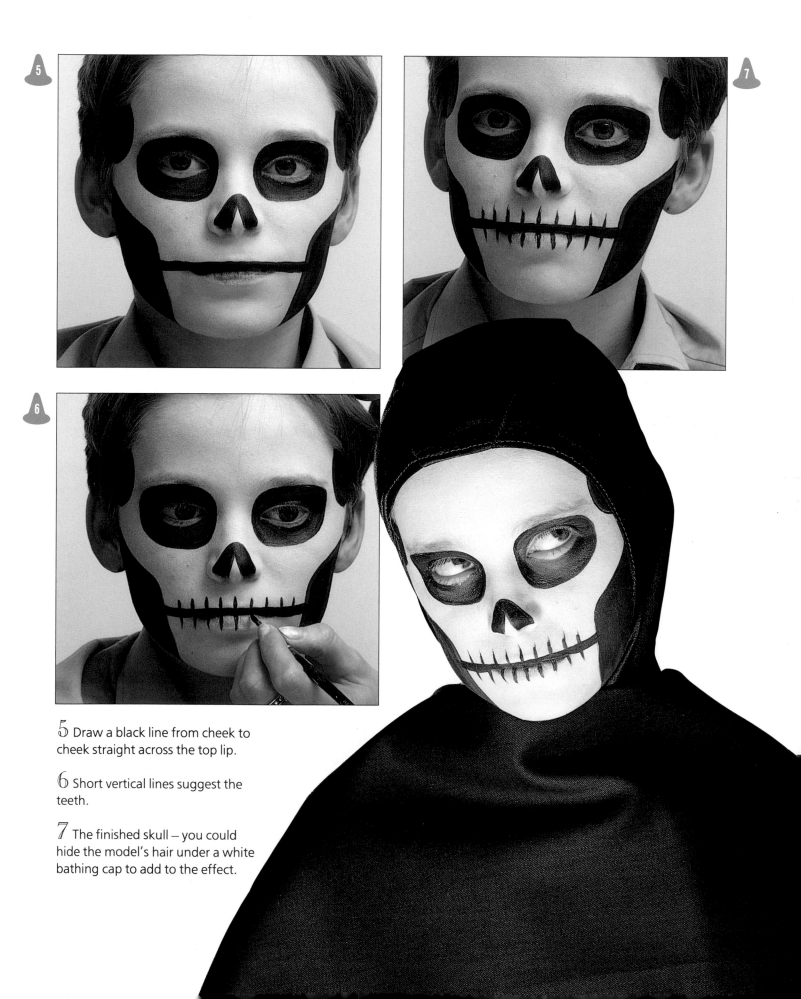

5 Draw a black line from cheek to cheek straight across the top lip.

6 Short vertical lines suggest the teeth.

7 The finished skull — you could hide the model's hair under a white bathing cap to add to the effect.

Dracula

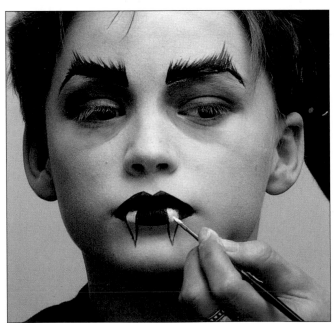

1 Cover the face with white, gently stippling over any patchy areas with a sponge. Add some angular black eyebrows, brushing upwards with light feathery brushstrokes.

2 Paint some grey over the top eyelid, round the inner corner of the eye and along the lower socket line. Blend the edges with a clean damp brush.

3 Draw the outline of long pointed fangs over the bottom lip, using a fine brush or a sharp black eye pencil.

4 Fill in the fangs in white and the surrounding lips in black.

5 Use a brush or a cotton bud to smudge some red paint along the lower eyelash line. The model should look up and away from you while you do this. Shade the cheek hollows with light grey using a sponge or a brush. Powder eye shadow could be used instead of paint, but powder colours are usually less dense than paint and do not last so long.

6 Add trickles of blood from the fangs and corners of the mouth.

Midnight Bat

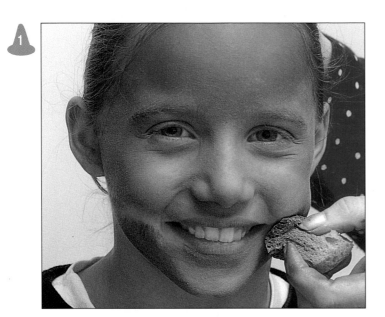

1 The base for this make-up consists of bands of colour stretching right across the face. Blend purple into blue and blue into green using the stippling technique described on page 11.

2 Draw the outline of the bat, starting at the top of the nose. Estimate where the points of each wing should fall and mark the place with a dot of paint – this will help you to make the shape symmetrical. Outline the eyes with a thin line in a feline shape that sweeps up at the outer corners and extends onto the nose slightly at the inner corners.

3 Fill in the bat shape in black, leaving the area round the eyes.

4 Use a fine brush to sketch the outlines of the moon and stars onto the forehead and cheeks.

5 Paint the area round the eyes in silver.

6 Fill in the moon in silver, and the stars in silver and gold. Add some horizontal streaks of silver around the moon to suggest a moonlit sky.

7 Decorate the stars and sky with glitter. The midnight bat is ready to fly.

4
SPECIAL EFFECTS

The use of special make-up to simulate blood, guts and gore has been used for many years in both the theatre and on film and the effects now achieved are sophisticated and horribly realistic, even under close scrutiny.

Now you have a chance to learn the tricks of the trade yourself. You will need a few bits of specialist equipment, such as wax and fake blood, available at theatrical suppliers, but the main ingredients are your imagination and ability to observe the gory world around you.

Try the projects in this chapter and then experiment with your own ideas – what about a wart made from puffed rice cereal – to shock your family and friends.

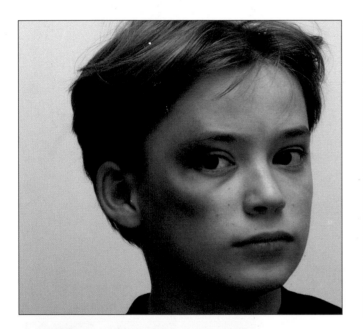

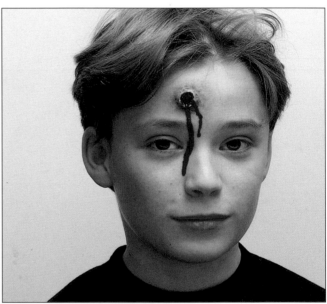

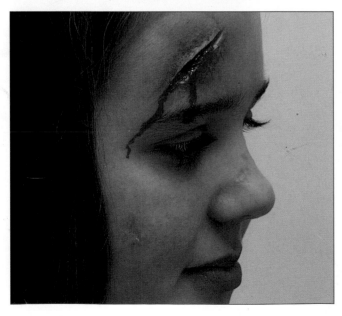

Black Eye

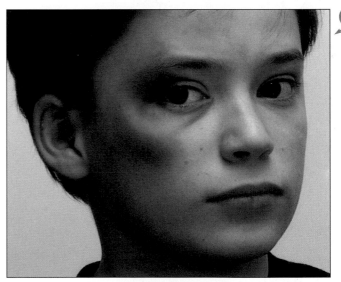

1 Mix dark red paint with a dash of grey and dab the colour over the outer eyelid and brow bone with your finger or a sponge. Using a brush, paint into the lower eye socket line at both the inner and outer corners of the eye. Blend the edges carefully with a cotton bud.

2 Feel for the cheekbone and dab some colour along the underside, fading out towards the temple.

3 Go back over the same areas with a touch of dark blue, allowing the colour to be a little heavier around the outer corner of the eye.

4 The finished black eye looks painfully realistic.

TIP: To make an eye look bloodshot, paint red along the inner rim.

5 For even more realism, add a small jagged red scar painted just above the eyebrow.

Bullet Hole

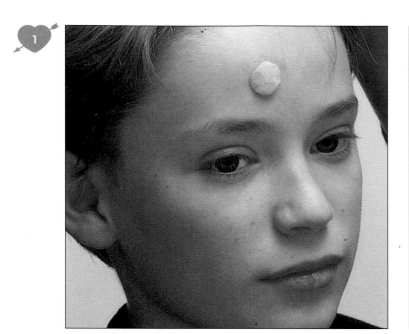

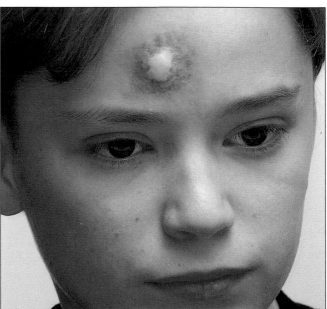

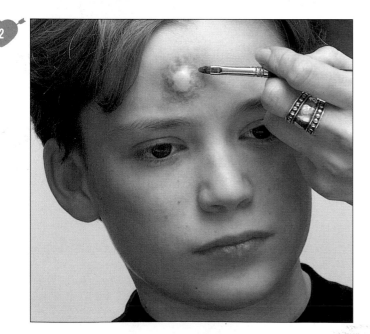

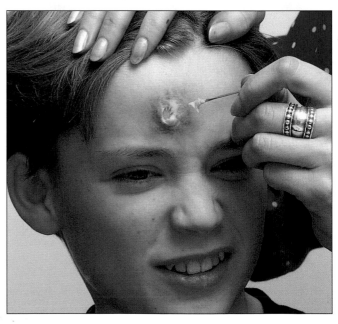

TIP: Don't handle wax for too long or it will become too soft and sticky to mould into shape.

1 Roll a small amount of wax into a ball and press it gently but firmly into place. Use a spatula or brush-end to blend the edges onto the skin.

TIP: A little cold cream used very sparingly will help to smooth and shape the edges.

2 Using a brush, colour the wax and the surrounding area in a dark red. Add a few dots of dark blue, blending the outer edges of the coloured areas

into the skin, but leaving the part closest to the wax slightly mottled.

3 At this stage the wax still looks like a lump on the skin.

4 Use a toothpick or orange stick to pick the centre of the wax away.

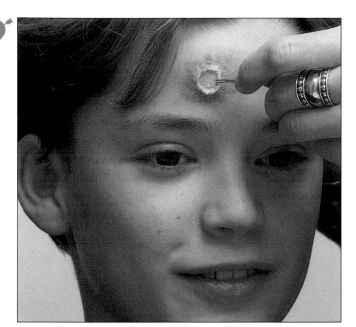

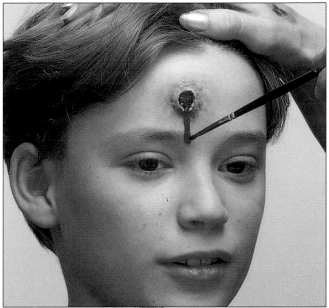

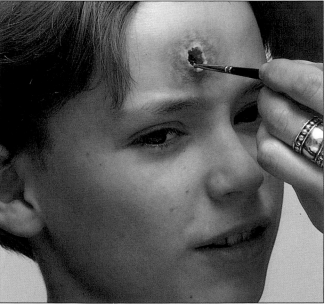

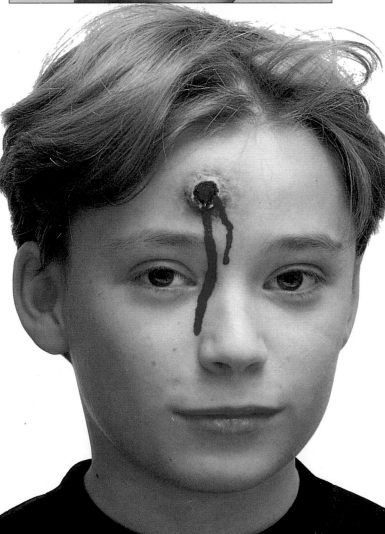

5 Create a hole, leaving the edges rough.

6 Paint the inside of the hole dark red and add some flecks of black randomly around the edge.

7 Apply plenty of fake blood. Take care not to get the fake blood on your clothes or the model's.

TIP: A blob of dark red jam in the hole adds depth and gore!

Open Cut

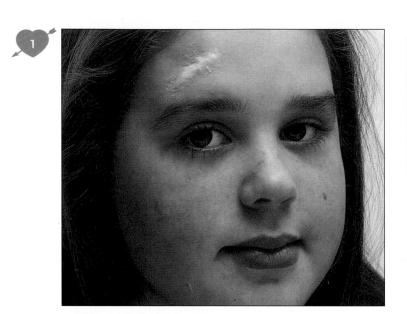

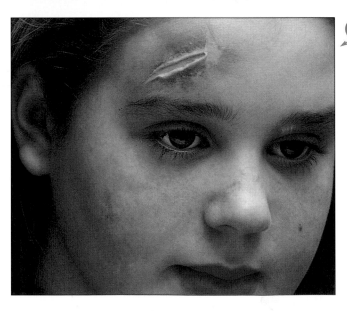

TIP: Avoid handling the wax too much, as it will become too soft and sticky to work with.

1 Mould a small amount of wax into the basic shape of the cut you are going to create. Press it gently onto the skin.

2 With a spatula or the back of your fingernail, shape and thin out the edges of the wax so that they blend onto the skin.

TIP: A tiny touch of cold cream will help to smooth out the edges.

3 With your finger or a small brush, lightly colour the wax and the surrounding area in dark red. A hint

of dark blue can be added to suggest bruising. The colours will look more effective if they are left mottled rather than blended together too much.

4 Pick away the wax to form the cut, using either the end of a spatula or brush, or a toothpick or orange stick.

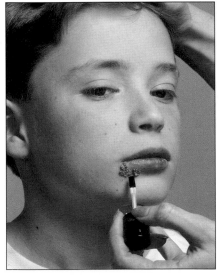

5 Line the centre of the cut with dark red using a fine brush. A few drops of fake blood help to make the cut look real.

TIP: If the fake blood appears too pink or orange mix in a little grey paint.

6 The finished wound.

Scab

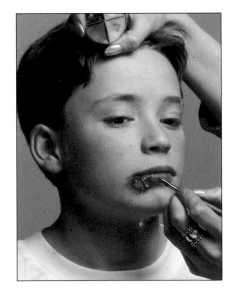

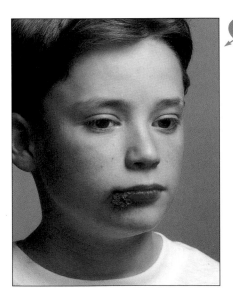

1 Crush a bran flake or cornflake into small pieces and stick them onto the skin using a tiny dab of surgical or water-soluble adhesive.

2 Discolour the area around the flakes by applying dark red with a brush, adding a few spots of grey/green here and there. Blend the edges of the colours into the skin with a cotton bud.

3 The finished scab.

TIP: The same method can be used with puffed rice to make very realistic warts and blisters.

Tattoos

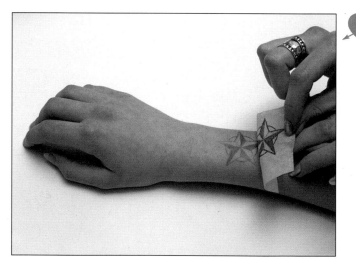

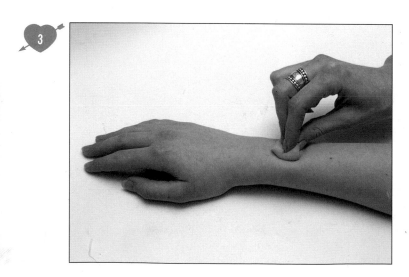

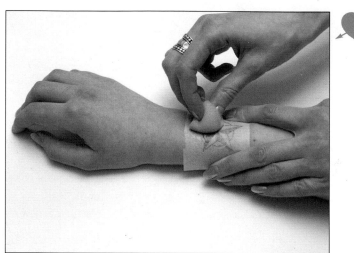

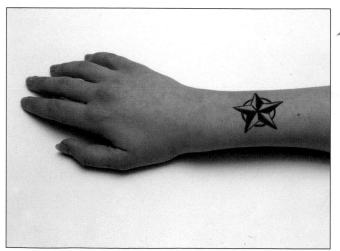

1 Trace your chosen design onto tracing paper or greaseproof paper.

2 Go over the outline with a very soft lead pencil, pressing very hard. If the design contains lettering, do this back to front so that the letters will eventually be the right way round.

3 Decide where the tattoo is to go, and dampen the area slightly.

4 Put the tracing pencil-shaded side down onto the skin and moisten the back with a sponge, holding the tracing very firmly in place.

5 Slowly pull back the paper. The design will have transferred to the skin.

6 The lines can be sharpened and areas filled with colour using paint or make-up pencils.

TIP: To avoid the risk of lettering appearing back to front you could add the letters directly onto the skin.

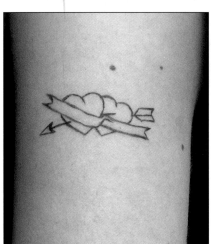

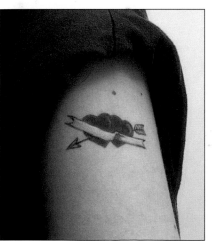

An example of a traditional tattoo, coloured with paint.

Some designs for you to trace or copy (see also Cheek Designs page 94).

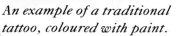

5
CARNIVAL

The word carnival is believed to be derived from the Latin words *carne* (meat) and *vale* (farewell). The word was first used for the celebrations that take place before the beginning of Lent – a period of fasting and penance in the Christian Church. There had been festivities at this time of year long before Christianity. Originally February was celebrated by the Ancient Greeks as the end of Harvest and to honour *Dionysus*, the God of wine, fruitfullness and vegetation. Similar celebrations were taken up by the Ancient Romans under the name *lupercalia*, referring to *Lupercas*, the God of flocks.

The connection between Carnival and masks derives from sacred rites performed at the start of the new farming season. The masks represented the souls of the dead who emerged to inspire fertility in the soil. These masks later became essential to the Carnival celebrations since they allowed all the party-goers, whether peasants or nobles, to go unrecognized as they took part in the wild street parties.

By shrouding our bodies in costume and paint we instil in ourselves a sense of invincibility and cast aside our inhibitions.

Batman

1 Paint the whole face yellow using a sponge.

2 Draw the outline of the bat in black, starting at the top of the nose. Estimate where the points of the wings should fall and mark the places with a dot of paint. This will help the design to be symmetrical.

3 Any mistakes within the outline will not show in the finished make-up.

4 Fill in the bat shape with black. Make sure the outline stays crisp, and take care when painting around the eyes.

Fairy Princess

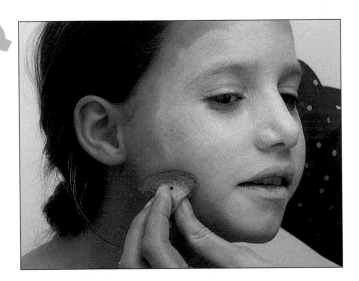

1

4

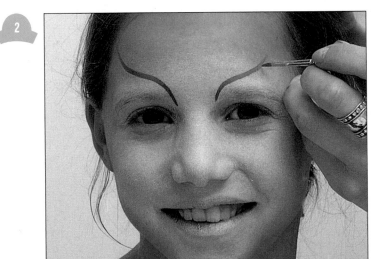

2

5

3

6

6 Enhance the natural shape of the lips with dark red. Decorate the cheeks with gold and add a star and other details to the forehead.

7 For an extra touch of magic, add some glitter to the star, leaves, lips and browlines.

1 Make a base of white, blending into a pink border. Use the stippling technique described on page 11.

2 Add thin purple eyebrows, sweeping the line up past the temples.

3 Paint the eyelids blue, starting just below the inner corner of the eye and winging the line up at the outer corner to echo the curve of the eyebrow line. Highlight the blue by painting gold along the top edge.

4 With the model's eyes closed, add a fine lilac line under the eye, starting below the inner corner and sweeping up following the same curve as the top line.

5 Using a very fine brush, design some delicate curls and leaves that descend from the lower eye lines.

Cowboy

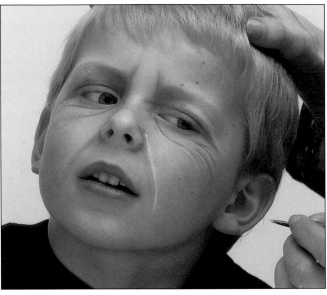

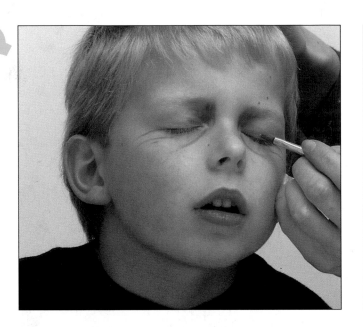

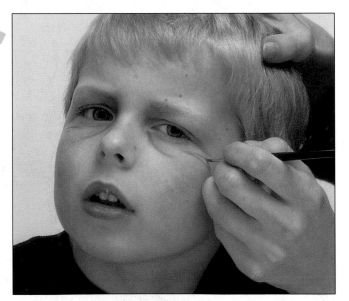

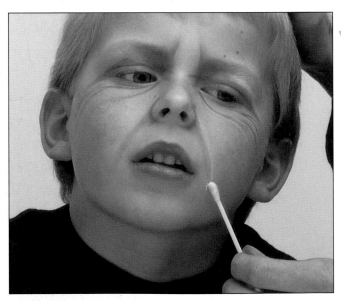

1 Using a thin brush and mid-brown paint, shade the eyelid and the inner corner of the eye, blending the colour down the sides of the nose slightly. Add a subtle line of colour to the lower part of the eye socket.

2 Add some wrinkle lines in their natural positions: downwards from the outer corner of the eye, from the nose down to the corners of the mouth, in the crease of the chin and across the forehead, as well as two vertical frown lines above the eyebrows.

3 Highlight the lines and wrinkles by painting a little white alongside them. To make the eyelids look droopy, paint a white diagonal line along the fold of the upper lid, starting at the eyebrow and ending below the outer corner of the eye.

4 Blend any hard edges using a slightly dampened cotton bud.

5 Create an unshaven look by stippling the beard and moustache area with a coarse sponge and some brown paint (see instructions on page 14). Build up the effect gradually, using only a small amount of colour. Dab the sponge on the back of your hand to remove any excess paint. Darken the eyebrows if necessary. This subtle make-up will enhance any cowboy fancy dress costume.

5

Rainbow

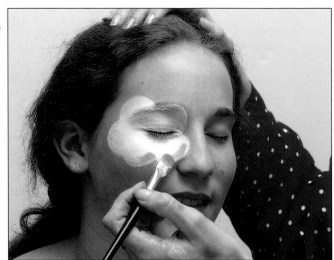

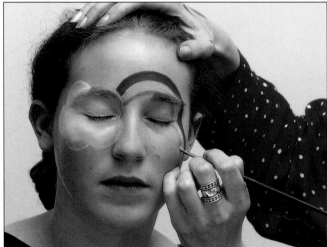

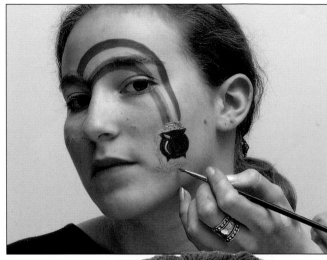

1 Paint the shape of a cloud in white over one eye and emphasize it with dashes of blue paint, blended into the white.

2 Paint the rainbow tapering down onto the cheek.

3 Draw a small black cauldron and paint a mound of gold brimming over the edge. Highlight the gold with flecks of glitter.

4 Finishing touches: pairs of curved strokes in black suggest birds flying over the cloud; add three small blue raindrops below the cloud; use a blend of red, yellow and orange to paint the sun behind the rainbow.

North American Indian

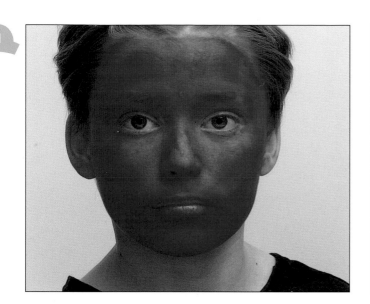

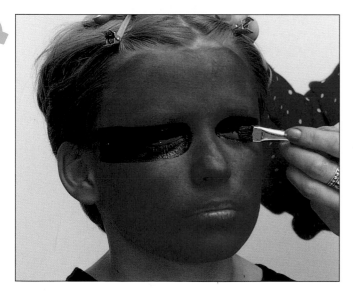

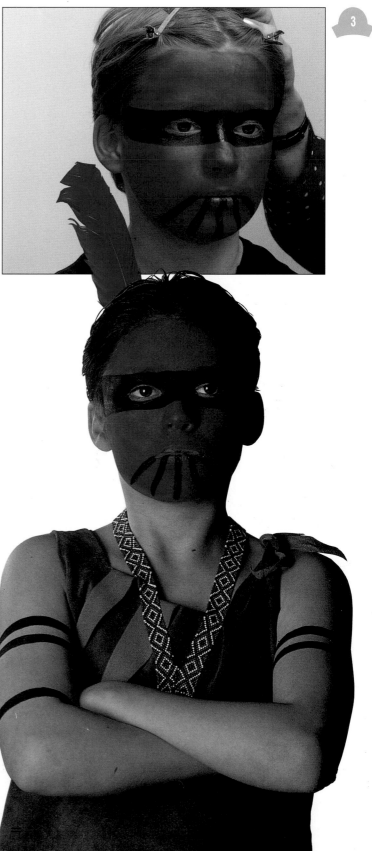

1 Paint the whole face red using a sponge.

2 Add a thick black stripe running straight across the face over the eyelids.

3 Finish the face with black lines from the bottom lip to the chin. The result looks very warlike.

TIP: The most effective Indian ritual masks use bold colours that traditionally represented the four directions: white for North; yellow for South; red for East; and black for West.

Pirate

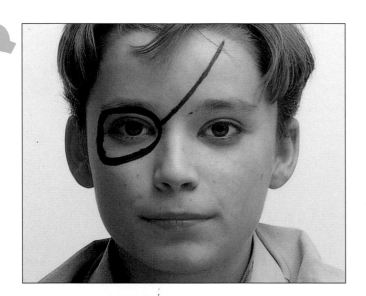

1 Draw the outline of the eye patch with a fine brush.

2 Fill in the outline with black and draw in the ties.

3 Create an unshaven look by stippling black paint gently onto the lower face with a sponge (see page 14 for full instructions).

TIP: Build up the colour gradually and don't overdo it.

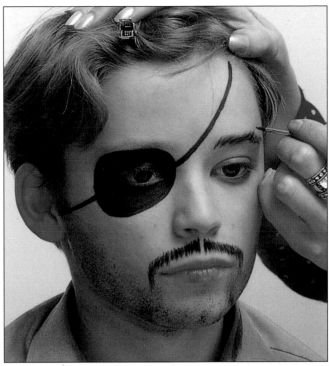

4 A realistic five o'clock shadow is beginning to emerge.

5 Paint on the moustache with a very fine brush using small sharp strokes.

6 Emphasise the model's eyebrows using the same sharp brush technique.

7 Create a scar by painting a thin dark red line and outlining it in white to achieve a 3-D effect. Paint on a few drops of fake blood.

Spiderman

1 Cover the face and neck with red paint using a sponge. Fill in the eye socket area above and below the eye in black.

2 Make a dot on the end of the nose and use this as a centre point to draw four thin black lines across the face:
1 right down the centre of the face;
2 straight across the face from ear to ear; 3 left to right diagonally from forehead to chin; and 4 right to left diagonally.

3 Begin to develop the web, starting near the centre and repeating the pattern at regular intervals.

4 The web continues right up to the edge of the face.

TIP: A spiderman costume would probably include a red hood but as the Aqua-Colours used here are easily washable you could gel the hair flat and continue the red paint over it.

Arabian Nights

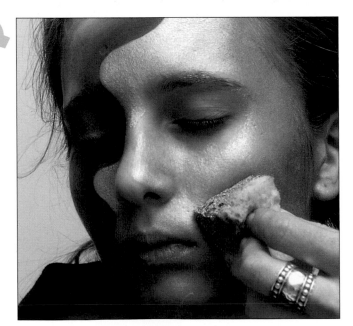

1 Paint a wavy line in purple from the centre of the forehead down onto the neck.

2 Outline the purple in gold. Use a brush along the edge to ensure a neat line, then fill in the rest of the face with gold.

3 Beside the purple, add a strip of pale blue following the same shape, then one of lilac before repeating the whole pattern starting again with purple.

4 Leave the outermost edges sharp, and blend all the other colours into each other using a wide flat brush.

5 The effect so far.

6 Shade the opposite eyelid in purple, fading it into blue on the brow bone. Colour the lips purple.

7 Dab gold glitter along the hard edges of the purple shapes, across the opposite eyebrow and over the lips.

Venetian Mask

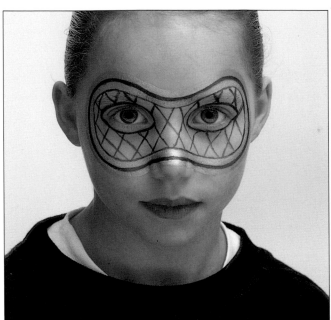

1 Sketch the outline of a mask onto the face with a grey eye pencil — make sure the shape is symmetrical. Outline the eyes in an almond shape. Trace over the grey outlines in black with a fine brush, or use a black eye liner.

2 Neatly paint a gold line around the inside and outside of the mask outline.

3 Carefully draw evenly spaced diagonal black lines across the mask in one direction only. Leave the shape marked out around the eyes blank. Repeat on the opposite diagonal.

4 Paint fine black triangles all round the edge of the mask to represent a frill.

5 Choose a diamond shape on one side of the mask, fill it with green and continue along the row across the face.

6 Miss a row, then colour another row green. Fill in the intervening rows with red. Paint the lips red and draw a whirly line extending from the mask down the sides of the face to represent ties.

Cheek Designs

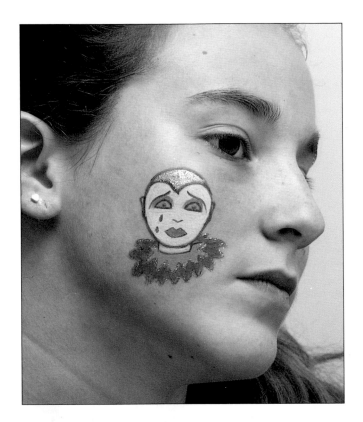

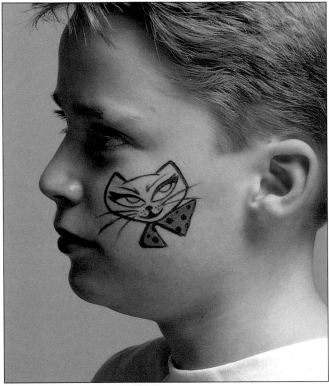

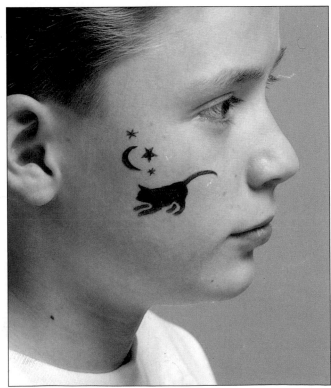

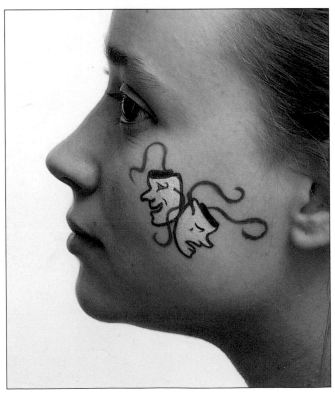

These little designs are quick and fun to do. Of course they don't have to go on your cheek – you could decorate your arms, legs, even your feet. Anything goes! The only basic rule to remember is that once you have drawn out the main outline, always apply the lightest colours first.

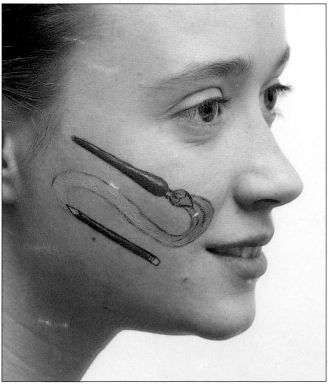

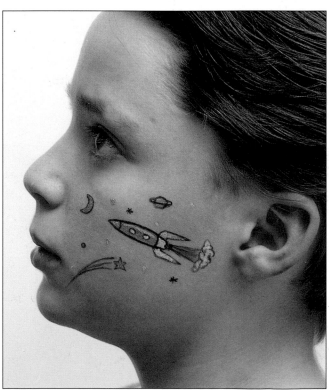

Appendix

Suppliers

The two major manufacturers of the water-based face paints used in this book are Kryolan and Grimas. To find a shop which carries the paints, either look up in the Yellow Pages under Theatrical Supplies or Make-up or contact one of the following:

KRYOLAN
Headquarters
Kryolan GmbH, Papierstrasse 10, D-W1000, Berlin 51, GERMANY

Charles H Fox Ltd
22 Tavistock Street, London WC2, UK

Kryolan Corporation
132 Ninth Street, San Francisco, CA 94103, USA

Backstage Theatrical
Shop 12, Upper Plaza, 95 Bourke Street, Melbourne, Victoria 3000, AUSTRALIA

Showface
12 Argyle Place, Millers Point, NSW 2000, AUSTRALIA

Selecon New Zealand Ltd
26 Putiki Street, Auckland 2, NEW ZEALAND

GRIMAS
Headquarters
Grimas, PO Box 3240, 2001 De Haarlem, The Netherlands

Treasure House of Make-up
197 Lee Lane, Horwich, Bolton, Lancashire BL6 7JD, UK

The Funny Shop
City Market, Bunda Street, Canberra, 2601 ACT, AUSTRALIA

Acknowledgements

SPECIAL THANKS TO:
Micky Fits, Sarah Jane Armstrong, Cliff Davis, The Museum of Mankind and Charles H Fox Ltd for supplying make-up.

THE MODELS

Hayley Andrews, Mitchell Andrews, Cheryl Benedettini, Becky Dewing, Victoria Dewing, Spencer Dewing, Chloé Faram, Jimmy Forrester, Laura Forrester, Heather Woods, Oliver Howe, Lisa Mare, Rachel Oliphant, Anya Paul and Clara Paul.

PICTURE CREDITS

Pictures for the gallery section on pages 6–8 were supplied by the following:
J Allan Cash Photolibrary: soldier, Chinese theatre.

Robert Harding Picture Library: Bahreini woman, Mount Hagen man, Toto the clown

"Cats" picture by Graham Brandon. Reproduced by kind permission of the V & A Theatre Museum, London